Irregular English Verbs

A systematic approach

by

Jakub Marian

First Edition, March 2018

ISBN: 978-1718787483

Printed by

On-Demand Publishing LLC, 100 Enterprise Way,
Suite A200, Scotts Valley, CA 95066, USA

(or one of its subsidiaries)

Before you start reading

You are reading the paperback version of this book. If you happen to have found this book freely available on the Internet (from an illegal source), please consider buying a legal copy (there is a PDF, Kindle, and paperback edition), which is also the only one guaranteed to be up to date. You can find links to all editions at

jakubmarian.com/irregular-english-verbs/

If you bought this book, you are allowed to make as many copies (electronic or physical) as you wish and distribute them to all members of your household. You are not allowed to make the book available publicly; if you wish to send it to someone not within your household, simply buy another paper or electronic copy.

If you find an error in the book, please send an email with a description of the error to

jakub.marian@jakubmarian.com

Table of Contents

Foreword

There are around 400 English verbs that have an irregular simple past tense or past participle and even more that manifest some form of irregularity in the present tense. Most books on irregular verbs simply list all irregular verbs in alphabetical order, with all their forms and a few examples of use.

This book takes a different approach, which is more suitable for people who want to read a book from cover to cover. Verbs are grouped together according to common patterns, such as a -d that becomes a -t in the past tense (e.g. bend, send), the pattern "-ink, -ank, -unk" (e.g. drink, sink), verbs that do not change at all (e.g. cut, put), etc.

Archaic verbs that are not used at all in modern English were not included in this book, but all irregular verbs that are for some reason still relevant were included, even if they are uncommon (such as "cleave" or "gainsay"), which, I hope, will allow you not only to master English verbs but also to expand your vocabulary in the course of reading this book.

— Jakub Marian
(author)

Irregularity in the present tense

There are a few English verbs that form the present tense in an irregular way. We will quickly discuss them before moving on to the past tense, which is the main source of difficulties.

The standard conjugation pattern (or, as linguists call it, "paradigm") followed by the vast majority of English verbs is as follows:

Infinitive: **to make**

I **make**	we **make**
you **make**	you (pl.) **make**
he/she/it **makes**	they **make**

Negative:
I/you/we/they **do not make** (**don't make**) he/she/it **does not make** (**doesn't make**)

Present participle: **making**

If a verb ends with one of the following sounds, the third person singular ending becomes **-es** (pronounced /ɪz/):

/s/, e.g. **kiss**: he kiss<u>es</u>, **miss**: he miss<u>es</u>
/ks/, e.g. **fix**: he fix<u>es</u>, **tax**: he tax<u>es</u>
/z/, e.g. **buzz**: it buzz<u>es</u>, **quiz**: he quiz<u>zes</u>
/ʃ/, e.g. **fish**: he fish<u>es</u>, **splash**: it splash<u>es</u>
/tʃ/, e.g. **catch**: he catch<u>es</u>, **watch**: he watch<u>es</u>

Notice that the third person singular of "quiz" is "quizzes", not "quizes". It is an instance of consonant doubling, which we will discuss in the next chapter.

If the verb ends in **-y** that is pronounced as /aɪ/, the ending is spelled "ies" instead of "ys", e.g.

fly: he fl<u>ies</u> /flaɪz/
supply: he suppl<u>ies</u> /səˈplaɪz/
fry: he fr<u>ies</u> /fraɪz/

If it ends in **-y** pronounced as /i/, the ending also becomes "ies", but the pronunciation is /iz/, e.g.

envy: he env<u>ies</u> /ˈɛnviz/
vary: it var<u>ies</u> /ˈvɛəriz/ (BrE), /ˈvɛriz/ (AmE),
embody: he embod<u>ies</u> /ɪmˈbɒdiz/ (BrE),
/ɪmˈbɑːdiz/ (AmE)

This spelling change does not apply when the final "y" is preceded by a vowel (and hence pronounced as /j/), e.g. **buy** (he buy<u>s</u>), **lay** (he lay<u>s</u>). All such verbs are regular in the present tense, except "say", which has an irregular pronunciation:

say: he say<u>s</u> /sɛz/ (not /seɪz/)

There are a few verbs ending in **-o** that becomes -oes in the third person singular (pronounced /əʊz/ in British English and /oʊz/ in American English):

go: he g<u>oes</u>
(the same applies to "go" with a prefix, e.g. "undergo", "forgo")
echo: it ech<u>oes</u>
veto: he vet<u>oes</u>
solo *(play a solo)*: he sol<u>oes</u>
radio *(send a message by radio)*: he radi<u>oes</u>
demo *(create a demo)*: he dem<u>oes</u>
lasso *(catch using a lasso)*: he lass<u>oes</u>

The verb "do" follows the same pattern in writing but has an irregular pronunciation:

> **do**: he d<u>oes</u> /dʌz/
> *(the same pronunciation pattern applies to "redo", "undo", and other similar verbs)*

VERBS "BE" AND "HAVE"

There are only two verbs (except modal verbs) that do not fall into any of the categories above. The verb "be" is completely irregular:

I **am** (I'**m**)	we **are** (we'**re**)
you **are** (you'**re**)	you (pl.) **are** (you'**re**)
he **is** (he'**s**)	they **are** (they'**re**)

Note that most native speakers pronounce "you're" identically to "your", which is why writing "your" instead of "you're" is one of the most common spelling mistakes. Similarly, "they're", "there" and "their" are pronounced identically ("y" is always silent in "they're").

"Be" is the only verb (except "have" and modal verbs, which we will discuss below) that does not form the negative using "do not" (it is not possible to say "I don't be"):

> I **am not** (**I'm not**)
> you **are not** (you**'re not**, you **aren't**)
> he **is not** (he**'s not**, he **isn't**)
> we/you/they **are not** (we**'re not**, we **aren't**)

There is no standard contraction of "am not" (the word "amn't" exists only in several Scottish dialects). In tag questions (which require a contraction), the expression "aren't I" is used instead:

> I am quite tall, **aren't** I?
> You are quite tall, aren't you?
> He is quite tall, isn't he?

This may seem strange at first, but saying "aren't I" has become fairly standard and is considered completely acceptable.

The verb "**have**" is in many ways similar to "be". Its third person singular is irregular, and the verb has its own contracted forms:

I **have** (I**'ve**)	we **have** (we**'ve**)
you **have** (you**'ve**)	you (pl.) **have** (you**'ve**)
he **has** (he**'s**)	they **have** (they**'ve**)

and its own negative forms:

> I/you/we/they **have not** (I**'ve not**, I **haven't**)
> he **has not** (he**'s not**, he **hasn't**)

Notice that the contracted form of "has" is the same as that of "is", so the intended meaning must be understood from the context.

The contracted forms of "have" are reserved for an auxiliary verb of the present perfect, e.g.

> I've got a car.
> (= *I have got a car.*)
>
> He's already left.
> (= *He has already left.*)

with the exception of a few set phrases, such as:

> I haven't the faintest idea.

(which is more common than "I don't have the faintest idea").

In spoken British English, contractions in other places are also considered acceptable:

> I've a fiver.
> (= *I have a £5 note. Acceptable in informal BrE.*)

Using the contracted forms of "have" in such a way in writing is generally considered bad style.

MODAL VERBS

There are 14 verbs in English that behave in a way that is completely different from all other verbs. They express concepts like possibility, ability, willingness, and commands. They differ from ordinary verbs in two ways.

The most important difference is that they cannot be combined with "do not" to create the negative (it is not possible to say, for instance, "he doesn't can"). The following list contains all English modal verbs together with their possible negative forms (forms labelled "dated" or "uncommon" should be avoided by non-native speakers):

can	– can not, cannot, can't
could	– could not, couldn't
may	– may, may not, *mayn't (dated)*
might	– might not, *mightn't (dated)*
shall	– shall not, shan't (only in BrE)
should	– should not, shouldn't
will	– will not, won't
would	– would not, wouldn't
must	– must not, mustn't
ought to	– ought not to, *oughtn't to (dated)*
had better	– had better not, hadn't better, 'd better not
dare*	– dare(s) not, don't dare, doesn't dare, *daren't (uncommon)*
need*	– need not, needn't, don't need, doesn't need *(see below)*
used to*	– didn't use to, used not to, *didn't used to (see below)*

The other way in which the verbs above differ from all other English verbs is that they do not get the ending -s in the third person singular:

> **can**: he can *(not "he cans")*
> **could**: he could *(not "he coulds")*
> **may**: he may *(not "he mays")*
> etc. *(except "dare" and "need", see below)*

The verb "**dare**" can be used in two different ways. In affirmative ("positive") clauses, it is usually used as an ordinary verb (usually, but not necessarily, with "to"):

> He dare̲s to challenge me.

It is possible to say "he dare challenge me", but such usage is rare in modern English. In negative clauses, it is mostly used as a modal verb:

> He dare not do that.

Nevertheless, the ordinary form "he doesn't dare to do" is completely acceptable.

In questions, again, both forms are possible:

> Dare you do that?
> Do you dare to do that?

but only the modal form is possible in the phrase "how dare you", as in "How dare you talk to me like that?"

The verb "need", similarly to "dare", is usually used as an ordinary verb in affirmative clauses and as either a modal verb or an ordinary verb in negative clauses:

> She needs to leave now.
> He need not do that.
> He does not need to do that.

Finally, "used to" is quite commonly negated as "didn't used to" in contemporary written English, but many people consider the combination of "did" and the -ed form of a verb wrong, so it is advisable to avoid it and use the more natural "didn't use to".

In questions, some speakers treat "used to" as any other modal verb and ask, for example, "Used he to go there?", while most find this construction unnatural. Treating "used to" as the past tense of an ordinary verb is the safest option (but note that it has no present-tense equivalent; "use to do" does not make sense in English).

The verbs "will" and "would" are special in that they have their own contracted forms:

> I'll, you'll, he'll, we'll, you'll (pl.), they'll
> I'd, you'd, he'd, we'd, you'd (pl.), they'd

The verb "had better" can be contracted to *'d better*:

> I**'d better**, you**'d better**, he**'d better**, etc.

It is important not to confuse the *'d* with the contracted form of "would". The correct way to expand *'d better* is virtually always "had better":

> You'd better go there.
> = You had better go there.
> *(not "you would better go there")*

Nevertheless, there are rare cases where "would better" is the correct option, namely when "better" is used as a verb meaning "to improve", e.g.

> If you did that, you'd better the lives of many people.

Final consonant doubling

As you surely know, the final consonant of some verbs gets doubled when the suffix -ing or -ed is added, e.g.

>**stop**: sto<u>pp</u>ing, sto<u>pp</u>ed
>**cram**: cra<u>mm</u>ing, cra<u>mm</u>ed

In other cases, it is not doubled:

>**visit**: visi<u>t</u>ing, visi<u>t</u>ed
>**shift**: shif<u>t</u>ing, shif<u>t</u>ed

The rule governing the doubling of the final consonant is actually quite simple. If a verb has just one syllable and ends with exactly **one vowel followed by one consonant (except "w", "x", and "y")**, the consonant is doubled:

rob: robbing, robbed
sit: sitting, (past tense: sat)
beg: begging, begged
hum: humming, hummed

If there are two vowels or two consonants at the end, no doubling occurs:

read: reading, (past tense: read)
coat: coating, coated
bark: barking, barked
fill: filling, filled

This applies also to "oo" and "ee":

cook: cooking, cooked
seed: seeding, seeded

Similarly, if a verb ends with a silent "e", do not double the preceding consonant:

take: taking, (past tense: took)
come: coming, (past tense: came)
hope: hoping, hoped
game: gaming, gamed

The letters "w" and "y" are never doubled (they act as vowels in this context):

snow: sno<u>w</u>ing, sno<u>w</u>ed
stay: sta<u>y</u>ing, sta<u>y</u>ed

Similarly, the letter "x" is never doubled, because it represents two consonants "ks":

box: bo<u>x</u>ing, boxed
vex: ve<u>x</u>ing, vexed

Words beginning with "qu" may seem like an exception to the rule, but "qu" is actually pronounced as "kw", i.e. as two consonants, which does not prevent the following vowel from doubling:

quiz: qui<u>zz</u>ing, qui<u>zz</u>ed (think of "kwiz")
quit: qui<u>tt</u>ing, qui<u>tt</u>ed (usually just "quit")

The rule can be summarized as:

> **One vowel + one consonant = doubling**
> *(in monosyllabic words; except -w, -x, -y)*

Polysyllabic words

The rule we described above ("one vowel + one consonant = doubling") applies only to monosyllabic words. Fortunately, it is not necessary to learn a separate rule for longer words; the same rule applies under the condition that the final syllable is stressed:

> **If the final syllable is stressed, apply the rule mentioned earlier. If not, do not double the final consonant.** *(Except when the final consonant itself is a verb and for -l British English, see below)*

Here are a few examples of verbs in which the final syllable is stressed and the rule ("one vowel + one consonant") applies (the stressed syllable is underlined):

prefer: pre<u>fer</u>ring, pre<u>ferred</u>
permit: per<u>mit</u>ting, per<u>mit</u>ted
rebel: re<u>bel</u>ling, re<u>belled</u>

If the final syllable is stressed but the original rule is not satisfied (there are either two consonants, two vowels, a silent "e", a "w", or a "y"), no doubling occurs:

insult: in<u>sult</u>ing, in<u>sult</u>ed
reboot: re<u>boot</u>ing, re<u>boot</u>ed
upgrade: up<u>gra</u>ding, up<u>gra</u>ded
survey: sur<u>vey</u>ing, sur<u>vey</u>ed
regrow: re<u>grow</u>ing, (past tense: re<u>grew</u>)

Finally, when the last syllable is not stressed, you do not have to think about the rule at all; the final consonant is not doubled:

visit: <u>vi</u>siting, <u>vi</u>sited
listen: <u>li</u>stening, <u>li</u>stened
happen: <u>hap</u>pening, <u>hap</u>pened
inherit: in<u>he</u>riting, in<u>he</u>rited
remember: re<u>mem</u>bering, re<u>mem</u>bered
develop: de<u>ve</u>loping, de<u>ve</u>loped

However, if the final syllable is itself a monosyllabic verb, it follows the normal rules for doubling, even when it is not stressed. For instance:

input: <u>in</u>putting, (*past tense: input*)
overrun: <u>over</u>running, (*past tense: <u>over</u>ran*)
eavesdrop: <u>eaves</u>dropping, <u>eaves</u>dropped
kidnap: <u>kid</u>napping, <u>kid</u>napped
worship: <u>wor</u>shipping, <u>wor</u>shipped

(because we would write "putting", "running", "dropping", "napping", and "shipping").

There is an important difference in **British English**: If the final consonant is an "l" preceded by a lone vowel, it is always doubled, even if the syllable is not stressed, e.g.

cancel: <u>can</u>celling, <u>can</u>celled
travel: <u>trav</u>elling, <u>trav</u>elled
model: <u>mod</u>elling, <u>mod</u>elled

This rule does not apply in **American English**, in which the words above would usually be spelled as:

cancel: <u>can</u>celing, <u>can</u>celed
travel: <u>trav</u>eling, <u>trav</u>eled
model: <u>mod</u>eling, <u>mod</u>eled

Of course, if the last syllable is stressed, the final "l" is doubled in British English as well as American English, e.g.

expel: exp<u>el</u>ling, exp<u>el</u>led

EXCEPTIONS

The world would be a nicer place if there were no exceptions to the rules. Unfortunately, even the rules outlined above have some exceptions, but if you apply the rules, you will be right in almost all cases (more than 99.9%).

Probably the two most notable exceptions are the words "format" and "program", which are stressed on the first syllable but still double the final consonant:

format: <u>for</u>matting, <u>for</u>matted
program: <u>pro</u>gramming, <u>pro</u>grammed

Verbs ending with a "c" are also slightly irregular (they insert an additional "k"):

panic: <u>pani</u>cking, <u>pani</u>cked
picnic: <u>pic</u>nicking, <u>pic</u>nicked
mimic: <u>mimi</u>cking, <u>mimi</u>cked

NOTE ON OTHER SUFFIXES

The rule we described applies in most cases when a suffix beginning with a vowel is added to a root. This includes the suffixes -er, -ar, and -or for verbs, e.g.

<u>rob</u>ber, **<u>beg</u>gar**, **<u>visi</u>tor**, **<u>wri</u>ter**
<u>tra</u>veller (BrE), **<u>tra</u>veler** (AmE)

or -al:

re<u>fer</u> – re<u>fer</u>ral
re<u>but</u> – re<u>but</u>tal
ap<u>prove</u> – ap<u>prov</u>al

but it also applies in other cases, including nouns, such as those with the suffix -ish:

snob – snobbish
red – reddish
fool – foolish
self – selfish

This rule alone can help you prevent a significant number of spelling errors in English.

Irregularity in the past tense

We have already mentioned one type of "irregularity" in the past tense—consonant doubling—which, ironically, only applies to so-called *regular verbs*, that is, verbs that form the past tense with the suffix -ed (or -d if the infinitive ends with an "e").

In this chapter, we will deal with verbs that do not form the past tense using the suffix -ed (or -d). They fall into many small groups of words that share some similarities.

How to read this chapter

One important attribute shared by virtually all irregular verbs is that **prefixes do not influence irregularity**. For example, the past tense of "pay" is "paid", and this form is always used in the past tense of "pay" with a prefix, e.g. "repaid", "prepaid", "overpaid". We will usually not mention verbs with prefixes in this book, unless they are irregular in a way different from the root verb, or it is hard to recognize the prefix.

To save space, verb forms will always be given in the following format (except the verbs "be" and "have" in the next section, which have more forms):

infinitive – past simple – past participle

For example, the verb "go" will be presented as

go – went – gone

Each section ends with a box captioned "Examples". It provides simple sentences containing the verbs presented in the given section, and I recommend reading the sentences once or several times just to see the verbs used in context.

Verbs "be" and "have"

The verb "be" is the only verb conjugated according to person in the simple past:

> *infinitive*: **to be**
>
> *past simple*:
>
> | | |
> |---|---|
> | I **was** | we **were** |
> | you **were** | you (pl.) **were** |
> | he/she/it **was** | they **were** |
>
> *past participle*: **been**

It never forms the negative using "did not". The only possible negative forms of the simple past are:

> I/he/she/it **was not** (**wasn't**)
> you/we/they **were not** (**weren't**)

The verb "**have**" is not conjugated according to person in the simple past, but it has its own contracted form:

> *infinitive*: **to have**
>
> *past simple*:
>
> | | |
> |---|---|
> | I **had** (I'**d**) | we **had** (we'**d**) |
> | you **had** (you'**d**) | you (pl.) **had** (you'**d**) |
> | he/she/it **had** (he'**d**) | they **had** (they'**d**) |
>
> *past participle*: **had**

The contracted form is used only in the past perfect, e.g.

> He'd gone before they arrived.

and in the modal verb "had better", which we have already discussed.

The negative form "**had not**" or "**hadn't**" is, again, used to form the past perfect:

> I hadn't left before they arrived.

It is not used in the literal sense, except in a few set phrases, such as

> I hadn't the faintest idea.

(which is more common than "I didn't have the faintest idea").

EXAMPLES

I *was* there yesterday. *Were* you there? How long has it *been*? It *wasn't* very interesting. There *weren't* many people.

I *had* a hamster. I*'d* left years before I graduated from high school. *Hadn't* you done that before I arrived?

ISOLATED CASES

There are several verbs that do not follow any clear pattern and have to be memorized in isolation. Those that have the same past simple and past participle are as follows:

dig – dug – dug
hold – held – held
hear – heard – heard
meet – met – met
sit – sat – sat
shoot – shot – shot
spin – spun – spun
stand – stood – stood *(incl. "understand")*
win – won /wʌn/ – won /wʌn/

Others have three different forms:

begin – began – begun
come – came – come
choose – chose – chosen
do – did – done
eat – ate – eaten
fall – fell – fallen
give – gave – given *(incl. "forgive")*
go – went – gone
run – ran – run
rise – rose – risen *(incl. "arise")*
see – saw – seen
slay – slew – slain
steal – stole – stolen
swim – swam – swum

There is not much more that can be said about these verbs. I recommend reading the sentences below several times to get used to these forms.

EXAMPLES

The dog *dug* a hole. It has *dug* out an old toy. He *held* the world record until last year. She has never *held* my hand. I *heard* you the first time! Have you *heard* the news? I *met* a nice girl. I've never *met* him. He *sat* in the car. I've never *sat* for so many hours.

They *shot* at the target. How many times have you *shot* at it? The car *spun* around several times. The spider has *spun* a huge web. I *stood* outside in the cold. Have you *understood* everything? She *won* a lottery! How much have you *won*?

The talk *began* five minutes ago. The show has *begun*. I *came* across an interesting book. I've *come* here to tell you the truth. The sun *rose* early this morning. The actor has *risen* to fame.

A storm *arose* during the night. These problems have *arisen* as a result of management failure.

I *did* it! What have you *done*? My cat *ate* my hamster. It hasn't *eaten* for a while. The book *fell* from the table. Many soldiers have *fallen* during the war. I *gave* it to a friend of mine. It was *given* to me by my father. She *forgave* me. Have you *forgiven* him? I *went* to the dentist. It has *gone* quite well.

They *ran* in the race. Why have you *run* away? I *chose* to become a teacher. It's the film we have *chosen*. I *saw* her face for the first time. Have you *seen* the film yet? He *swam* in the lake. He has *swum* quite far away [note: the present perfect of "swim" is rarely used]. The knight *slew* the dragon. The dragon was *slain* by the knight. Corrupt politicians *stole* tax money. How much have they *stolen*?

MORE COMPLEX ISOLATED CASES: CLOTHE, SHOE, SPIT, SHINE, SWELL, BID

The verb "clothe", meaning "to dress" or "to provide clothes", can be either regular or irregular:

clothe – clothed or clad – clothed or clad

"Clothed" is more common than "clad" in the past simple, but both forms of the past participle are common.

The verb "shoe", which means "to provide shoes" or to "put shoes on someone or something", is irregular:

shoe – shod – shod

For example, it is possible to say:

He was badly *clad* and *shod*.

Another meaning of the verb "shoe" is "to put a horseshoe on a horse". For example:

The horses were sent to the stables to be *shod*.

The verb "spit" has two possible forms in American English:

spit – **spat** or **spit** (AmE) – **spat** or **spit** (AmE)

The irregular form ("spat") is more common in American literature than "spit" and more than ten times as common in British literature, so I recommend using it.

The verb "shine" has two principal meanings. When it means "to produce light", it follows the following pattern:

shine (produce light) – **shone** – **shone**

For example:

The moon *shone* above our heads.

However, when it means "to polish something to make it bright", it is regular:

shine (polish, e.g. shoes) – **shined** – **shined**

For instance:

He *shined* his shoes every morning.

In the sense of aiming a source of light at something, the verb is often used as a regular verb in American English:

He *shone* (or *shined* in AmE) his flashlight on his face.

Such usage is less common in British English.

The verb "**swell**" has a possible irregular past participle:

swell – swelled – swelled or **swollen**

Both "has swelled" and "has swollen" are common as the present perfect of "swell", but when the past participle is used as an adjective, it is virtually always "swollen", as in

My eyelids are often *swollen* in the morning.

Finally, the verb "**bid**" in the sense of either issuing a command or uttering a greeting is the only verb (except verbs derived from it) following the "pattern" -id -ade -idden in the past tense:

bid (e.g. farewell) – **bade** – **bidden**

Traditionally, only the form above was used. However, in modern English, this pattern is often replaced by:

bid – **bid** – **bid**

and the traditional pattern is never used when talking about bidding in an auction. For example:

> She bade/bid me farewell.
> He bid £2,000 on the painting.
> (*Not possible: "he bade £2,000"*)

The verb "forbid", which is derived from "bid", follows the traditional pattern:

forbid – **forbade** – **forbidden**

EXAMPLES

They *clothed* the poor [using "clad" as the past simple is uncommon]. She was *clothed* (or *clad*) in white.

The smith *shod* the horse. He has *shod* many a horse.

The angry mob *spat* (or *spit* in AmE) on the thief. They have *spat* (or *spit* in AmE) on him.

The sun *shone* brightly while I *shined* my shoes. The sun has *shone* for billions of years.

My hand *swelled* up after an insect bite. It has *swollen* (or *swelled*) quite a lot.

The princess *bade/bid* him farewell. The king *bade/bid* [asked] her to follow him. She was *bidden/bid* to enter. I *forbade* you to eat that! It is *forbidden* to smoke here.

Peter *bid* a lot of money in the auction yester-day. Have you *bid* on any item yet?

THE VERB "GET"

The verb "get" has two forms of the past participle:

get – got – got or gotten

Only "**got**" is used as the past participle of "get" in **British English**; if you learn British English, avoid the form "gotten" altogether.

However, the situation is more complex in **American English**. In the sense of "**receive**" or "**become**", the past participle is usually "gotten", e.g.

> I have never gotten a gift.
> (= *I have never received a gift.*)

> I've gotten interested in chess.
> (= *I've become interested in chess.*)

In the sense of "**have**" (possess) or "**must**", the past participle is always "got":

> She's got five children.
> (= *She has five children*)

> I've got to go.
> (= *I must go.*)

Sometimes both forms are possible but express different ideas:

> I've got a lot of questions.
> (= *I have a lot of questions.*)
>
> I've gotten a lot of questions.
> (= *I've received a lot of questions.*)

The verb "get" has around 30 different meanings, and covering the usage of each of them would be beyond the scope of this book. As a rule of thumb, if the meaning is unrelated to possession or necessity, the preferred form is "gotten" (but both forms are possible in many cases).

Even though the verb "**forget**" was derived from "get" by adding the archaic prefix for-, it does not follow the distinction above and is always used as follows:

forget – forgot – forgotten

Some native speakers use "forgot" as the past participle, but such usage is usually considered obsolete (it was common in the 18th and 19th century).

"**Beget**", another verb derived from "get" meaning "to become a father of" or "to be the source of", has two possible past simple forms:

beget – begat or begot – begotten

It is rarely used in modern English, but it is quite common in historical and religious context and in certain phrases, such as "violence begets violence".

EXAMPLES

(To practice the forms "got" and "gotten", read the examples at the beginning of this section.)

I *forgot* your number. Have you already *forgotten* it?

Isaac *begat* Jacob. Violence has always *begotten* violence [note that the present perfect of "beget" is rarely used].

Verbs with invariant past tense

There is a huge class of verbs that are the same in the past tense as in the infinitive, e.g. set, cut, hit. This means is that you have to recognize from the context whether the past tense or the present tense is intended. You could say both:

> They cut vegetables every day. [present tense]

and

> They cut vegetables yesterday. [past tense]

If the verb is in the third person singular, you can recognize the past tense by the absence of the third-person ending -s:

> He cut vegetables. [past tense]
> He cuts vegetables. [present tense]

Since the list of such verbs is very extensive and all three past forms of each verb are the same, we will change the usual format and show every verb together with an example sentence in the third person singular (the subject will be either "he", "she", or "it"), and there will be no examples at the end of this section.

This should make remembering the verbs easier. We will also list common verbs with prefixes that are harder to recognize. Here is the list:

- **bet** – He bet on a good horse.

- **bid** (offer amount) – He bid a lot of money.

  Note: In other senses of "bid" (e.g. "bid farewell"), the pattern "bid – bade – bidden" is more common.

- **broadcast** – He broadcast the good news.

  Note: Most dictionaries list also "broadcasted" as a possible form, but this form is not commonly used in practice.

- **burst** – She burst out laughing.

- **cut** – He cut some vegetables.

- **cost** – It cost a lot.

- **cast** – Frodo cast [threw] the ring into the fire, didn't he?

- **fit** – It fit(ted) into the box.

  In the US, the past tense and past participle are usually "fit", whereas in the UK they are usually "fitted". However, when used as adjectives, "fit" means healthy or appropriate, and "fitted" means designed to fit, both in the US and in the UK.

- **forecast** He forecast good weather.

  Even though the form "forecasted" exists, "forecast" is much more common.

- **fraught** (only used in the past participle in the sense of "filled", "loaded") – The situation was fraught with danger.

  "To fraught" means "to load". However, it is only used as an adjective in modern English.

- **hit** – The ball hit me.

- **hurt** – It really hurt.

- **input** – He input the figures into a spreadsheet.

  Some dictionaries allow the alternative "inputted", but this alternative is uncommon in published literature. Probably the most sensible recommendation is to avoid using "input" as a verb altogether and use a suitable synonym, such as "enter", "insert", or "type".

- **knit** – My grandma knit(ted) a scarf.

  Both "knit" and "knitted" are acceptable, but the regular form is more common.

- **let** – Who let the dogs out?

- **offset** [compensate] – It offset the costs.

- **put** – She put a coin into the tip jar.

- **quit** – He quit his job.

- **reset** – She reset the settings.

- **retrofit** – He retrofit(ted) the car with an improved engine.

  Note: "to retrofit" means "to equip something with a part it didn't originally have". The same note as for "fit" applies here.

- **rid** [remove something causing a problem] – The hero rid our streets of crime.

- **set** – She set a new world record.

- **shed** – It shed some light on the issue.

- **shit** (vulgar) – The dog shit/shat on the floor.

The form "shat" is less common.

- **shut** – He shut down the computer.

- **slit** [make a cut] – The knife slit his vein.

- **sublet** ["sub-rent"] – He sublet his room to another person.

- **spread** – It spread from one region to another.

- **thrust** [push quickly] – She thrust her hands into her pockets.

- **typeset** – Who typeset this book?

- **upset** – It upset me.

- **wed** ["to marry", old-fashioned] – A rock star wed(ded) a top model.

  The form "wedded" has traditionally been more common, but the irregular form "wed" is more common in modern English.

- **wet** – The baby wet the bed.

  Both "wet" and "wetted" are in use, but the regular form is considered unnatural by many speakers.

The verb "read" follows the same pattern in writing but not in pronunciation:

- **read** /riːd/ – He read /rɛd/ the article. I haven't read /rɛd/ it yet.

Finally, the past tense of "beat" is also "beat", but the past participle is "beaten":

- **beat** /biːt/ – She beat /biːt/ me in the game. I have never beaten /biːtn/ her.

Using "beat" as the past participle is somewhat common in speech, but it is usually considered colloquial.

Two miniature patterns
-ELL -OLD AND
-AKE -OOK -AKEN

There are two "miniature" patterns consisting of just two verbs each (not counting prefixes):

sell – sold – sold
tell – told – told

forsake – forsook – forsaken
take – took – taken *(incl. "partake")*

Note that "forsake" means "abandon someone when you have a responsibility to stay", and it is found especially in religious and historical contexts. "Partake in something" means "to take part in something", and "partake on something" means "eat or drink something that is offered" (both meanings are rather old-fashioned).

EXAMPLES

The dealer sold me a new car. They have sold a lot of cars already. They *told* me the price beforehand. Have I *told* you about it?

They all *forsook* him and fled. Father, why have you *forsaken* me? They *took* it away from me. Have you *taken* your medication today? He unwillingly *partook in* [took part in] the social life

---

of the town. He has *partaken of* [consumed] the
food provided to every monk.

PAST TENSE WITH -T
INSTEAD OF -ED

There is a large class of verbs that get the suffix -t
instead of -ed in the past tense, sometimes with another minor change (mostly the substitution /iː/
→ /ɛ/ in the root of the verb):

> creep – crept – crept
> deal – dealt /dɛlt/ – dealt /dɛlt/
> dwell [live somewhere] – dwelt* – dwelt*
> feel – felt – felt
> keep – kept – kept
> kneel – knelt* – knelt*
> lose – lost – lost
> mean – meant – meant
> sweep – swept – swept

Note that while the forms "dwelled" and "kneeled" exist, the forms with -t are much more common, and I recommend sticking to them.

When forming the past tense and the past participle of the verbs listed below, we can choose freely between the irregular form (with -t) and the regular form (with -ed). I recommend using the regular (-ed) form in writing. The -t form may be perceived as "too British" by Americans, whereas the -ed form is perfectly acceptable in the UK:

> **burn** – **burned** or **burnt**
> **dream** – **dreamed** /driːmd/ or **dreamt** /drɛmt/
> **lean** – **leaned** /liːnd/ or **leant** /lɛnt/
> **leap** – **leaped** /liːpt/ or **leapt** /lɛpt/
> **learn** – **learned** or **learnt**
> **smell** – **smelled** or **smelt**
> **spell** – **spelled** or **spelt**
> **spill** – **spilled** or **spilt**
> **spoil** – **spoiled** or **spoilt**

EXAMPLES

The finals *crept* closer every day. Many non-standard forms have *crept* into the English language. She *dealt* with the problem quite well. Have you *dealt* with it? They *dwelt* ["lived", formal] in a small castle near the sea. They have *dwelt* there since the 15th century. I *felt* bad about it. I have always felt this way.

She *kept* it a secret. The climate has *kept* tourists away. The knight knelt before the king. Has he *knelt* yet? He *lost* his keys. I am completely *lost*. It *meant* a lot to us. It has never *meant* a lot to me. She *swept* the crumbs off the table. They were *swept* away by the waves.

Past tense with -d replaced by -t

When a verb ends with a -d, it is sometimes replaced by -t in the past tense. There are 6 such verbs:

> **bend – bent – bent**
> **build – built – built**
> **lend – lent – lent**
> **rend** [to tear apart forcefully] – **rent – rent**
> **send – sent – sent**
> **spend – spent – spent**

Note that the verb "**gild**", which is a literary word meaning "to cover a surface with a thin layer of gold or a substance that looks like gold", has two possible forms: gilded (more common) or gilt (less common).

PATTERNS -ING -ANG -UNG AND -INK -ANK -UNK

There is a class of irregular English verbs that follow the pronunciation pattern /ɪŋ/ → /æŋ/ → /ʌŋ/ in the past tense, two of which end with "-ing" in the present tense:

> **ring** /rɪŋ/ – **rang** /ræŋ/ – **rung** /rʌŋ/
> **sing** /sɪŋ/ – **sang** /sæŋ/ – **sung** /sʌŋ/

Notice that the "g" at the end is not pronounced. The /ŋ/ sound found at the end of these words is produced simply by making the back of your tongue touch the back of your throat.

There are four other verbs that follow the same pattern but end with a "k", which *is* pronounced:

> **drink** /-ıŋk/ – **drank** /-æŋk/ – **drunk** /-ʌŋk/
> **shrink** /-ıŋk/ – **shrank** /-æŋk/ – **shrunk** /-ʌŋk/
> **sink** /sıŋk/ – **sank** /sæŋk/ – **sunk** /sʌŋk/
> **stink** /stıŋk/ – **stank** /stæŋk/ – **stunk** /stʌŋk/

The simple past of "**stink**" can, alternatively, be "**stunk**", but this is somewhat less common.

EXAMPLES

The name *rang* a bell. Your phone has *rung*. She *sang* a beautiful song. The song was *sung* by a professional singer.

I *drank* three beers yesterday. Almost all water was *drunk*. The T-shirt *shrank* during the first wash. Titanic *sank* in the morning of 15 April 1912, but it wasn't *sunk* by a submarine; it collided with an iceberg. The cheese *stank* (or

---

stunk) like a dirty sock, and the kitchen has *stunk* for hours after dinner.

PATTERN -AY -AID -AID

Most English learners are well aware of the pattern -ay/-aid of irregular English verbs. However, this is more the exception than the rule. There are only 3 verbs (not counting prefixes) that follow the pattern:

> **lay – laid – laid**, pronounced /leɪd/
> **say – said – said**, pronounced /sɛd/
> **pay – paid – paid**, pronounced /peɪd/

Verbs with prefixes, follow the same pattern, but note that the verb "relay" in the sense "to receive or send information" is unrelated to "lay" and is regular (relay – relayed – relayed). Of course, if the intended meaning of "relay" is "lay again", the past tense and participle are "relaid".

The verb "gainsay" (meaning "contradict, deny") follows the same pattern as "say" (including pronunciation): **gainsay – gainsaid – gainsaid**. This is because gain- is an uncommon prefix meaning "against".

Pay attention to the verb "slay", which looks similar but is completely irregular:

slay – slew – slain

All other verbs ending with "ay" are regular, for example:

essay – essayed – essayed
play – played – played
stay – stayed – stayed
[… and many others]

EXAMPLES

He *said* /sɛd/ it. She *laid* /leɪd/ him on the bed. I *repaid* /rɪˈpeɪd, riːˈpeɪd/ my debts. The facts cannot be *gainsaid* /ˌɡeɪnˈsɛd/ [disputed, contradicted]. They *relaid* [laid again] the floor

---

tiles. The message was *relayed* [broadcast] by radio.

The knight *slew* the dragon. The dragon was *slain* by the knight.

Examples of similar regular verbs: We *played* a game. She *stayed* at home. He *essayed* a smile. The T-shirt *frayed* [the threads in the fabric started to come apart].

Verbs "lie" and "lay"

The verbs "lie" and "lay" are perhaps the two most confusing irregular English verbs. "Lie" has two fundamentally different meanings: "not to tell the truth" and "to be in a horizontal position" (or "to be located somewhere"). "Lay" means "to put something in a particular position"—that is, after you lay something somewhere, it lies there.

So far, so good, but when we start using these verbs in the past tense, things get confusing. "Lie" in the sense of not telling the truth (and *in this sense only*) is regular:

lie (not tell the truth) – **lied** – **lied**

In *all other senses*, "lie" follows the pattern

lie (be located/horizontal) – **lay** – **lain**

As you can see, "lay" has two meanings. "I lay" can mean either "I was in a horizontal position" (the past tense of "lie") or "I put something somewhere" (the present tense of "lay").

Which meaning is intended should always be clear from the context because "lie" is never used with an object (you cannot "lie something") and "lay" is never used without one (you always "lay something"). There is a tendency among native speakers to say "laying" instead of "lying", e.g. "I was laying in bed", but this is widely considered incorrect.

The distinction is also clear in the third person singular: "he lays" is the present tense of "lay", while "he lay" is the past tense of "lie".

There are two more verbs that are derived from "lie" in the latter sense and thus follow the same pattern: underlie – underlay – underlain; overlie – overlay – overlain.

The verb "lay" itself, which we have already mentioned in the previous section, is conjugated as

lay – laid – laid

Pay special attention to words like "overlay" and "underlay", which may be either past-tense forms derived from "lie" or present-tense forms derived from "lay".

EXAMPLES

He *lied* on his résumé. Have you ever *lied* to someone?

The cabin *lay* [was located, from "lie"] in the woods. He has *lain* [was horizontal, from "lie"] on the meadow for hours.

Hens *lay* eggs [present tense of "lay"]. They *laid* lots of eggs [past tense of "lay"]. How many have they *laid*?

The principle of constant speed of light *underlay* [was the basis of; past tense of "underlie"] the foundation of the theory of relativity. They have to *underlay* [lay under; present tense] the cover with a water-resistant material; they *underlaid* it.

The layer of sediment *overlay* [was above; from "overlie"] a large area of bedrock. The workers *overlay* [cover, put on top; present tense] wood with gold; they *overlaid* it with gold.

VERBS WITH -OUGHT AND -AUGHT

A moderately large class of irregular English verbs are characterized by having /ɔːt/ in their pronunciation in the past tense and past participle. In most cases, /ɔ:t/ is spelled "ought":

> **bring – brought – brought**
> **buy – bought – bought**
> **fight – fought – fought**
> **seek – sought – sought**
> **think – thought – thought**

There are two more verbs following the same pattern but with /ɔ:t/ being spelled as "aught":

> **catch – caught – caught**
> **teach – taught – taught**

Furthermore, the verb "beseech" (a literary word meaning "to beg for something in an anxious way") traditionally follows the same pattern, but it is also often used as a regular verb in modern English (in the rare cases when it is used at all):

> **beseech – besought** or **beseeched –**
> **– besought** or **beseeched**

EXAMPLES

He *bought* the girl a flower and *brought* her home. Firefighters *fought* a fire. They *sought* a source of water. I *thought* about that.

The fisherman *caught* a fish. It *taught* him a lesson.

They *besought* Jesus not to go up to Jerusalem. [Only the form "besought" is found in classical translations of the Bible, but modern prose imitating a classical style may choose freely between "beseeched" and "besought".]

PATTERN -ING -UNG -UNG AND THE VERB "HANG"

There are six verbs that follow the pattern -ing -ung -ung:

cling [hold on tightly] – **clung** – **clung**
sling [put by force] – **slung** – **slung**
sting [puncture skin] – **stung** – **stung**
string [attach strings] – **strung** – **strung**
swing [rock, dangle] – **swung** – **swung**
wring [twist and squeeze] – **wrung** – **wrung**

"Hang" follows a similar pattern:

hang – **hung** – **hung**

However, in the sense "to kill by hanging", the verb is regular:

They hang<u>ed</u> the criminals.
(*Not: "They hung the criminals."*)

EXAMPLES

He *clung* to the lifebuoy above his sunken boat. He has *clung* to it for hours, desperately awaiting help. The wasp *stung* me! I was *stung* by a wasp. He *strung* the guitar himself. The guitar was *strung* recently. The warrior *swung* his sword above his head. The pendulum has

---

swung several times. I *wrung* the wet towel. He has *wrung* the cloth out dry [note: the past participle of "wring" is rarely used].

An old chandelier *hung* above the table. It has *hung* there for centuries. Criminals were commonly *hanged* up until the 20th century.

PATTERN -IND -OUND -OUND

There are four verbs following this pattern:

> **bind – bound – bound**
> **find – found – found**
> **grind – ground – ground**
> **wind** /waɪnd/ – **wound – wound**

"Wind", when it is pronounced /waɪnd/, means "to have many bends and twists", as in

> The path winds /waɪndz/ down the mountain.

or "to twist something around itself or something else", e.g.

> He wound the wool into a ball.

When it is pronounced /wɪnd/, it can be used as a relatively uncommon verb meaning "to make somebody unable to breathe easily", which is regular and mostly used in the passive:

> The boxer was winded /wɪndɪd/ by a blow to the stomach.

EXAMPLES

They *bound* his hands together. The book comes in three volumes *bound* in leather. I *found* a penny. They haven't *found* out yet. The miller *ground* the grain. You can buy *ground* pepper in a supermarket. After I finished listening to music, I *rewound* the tape. She has *wound* up in a hospital [note: "wind up", meaning "end up", is informal].

Verbs with -ide and -ite (and -ight)

The verbs that end with -ide or -ite form a relatively heterogeneous group. They share some similarities but also many subtle differences. Let's go through all of them, one by one.

"Hide" and "bite" shorten the vowel and receive an -en in the past participle:

> **hide – hid – hidden**
> **bite – bit – bitten**

Somewhat similar and yet different are "slide" and "light":

> **slide – slid – slid**
> **light – lit – lit**

The participle "slidden" was in use in the 19th century, but it is now considered obsolete.

The vowel "i" commonly changes to "o" in -ite and -ide verbs:

write – wrote – written
smite [hit, strike, kill] **– smote – smitten**
stride – strode – stridden or **strode**
ride – rode – ridden

The verb "smite" is uncommon in modern English (it is used only in historical and religious contexts). However, the past participle "smitten" is used figuratively as an adjective meaning "suddenly feeling in love with", e.g.

He was completely smitten by her.

The verb "abide" (except the phrasal verb "abide by", as we well see below) does not get the suffix -en in the past participle:

abide (live, endure) **– abode – abode**

"Abide" is a literary expression meaning "to stay or live in a place" or to "endure or bear". It is rarely used in modern English.

However, it still has its place in contemporary English as a phrasal verb "abide by (a rule or agreement)" in the sense of "accept", "respect", as in "the players must abide by the rules".

In this case, it is conjugated as a regular verb:

abide by ... – **abided** by ... – **abided** by ...

There is one more archaic verb of interest that follows a similar pattern as the verbs above: *hagride*. It means "to afflict with worry or dread", and it follows one of two possible patterns:

hagride – **hagrode** – **hagridden** or
hagride – **hagrid** – **hagrid**

While the verb itself is not commonly used in practice, the latter form is interesting in that it is the source of the name of Hagrid from J. K. Rowling's Harry Potter universe.

EXAMPLES

The child *hid* in the woods. She has *hidden* it from our sight. Charlie *bit* me. Has he *bitten* you many times?

His hand *slid* away from her. Half of our supplies had *slid* into the river during a flood. She *lit* a candle. The streets were inadequately *lit*.

She *wrote* a letter to me. I've *written* a book! He *smote* [killed] all the first-born of Egypt. He was completely *smitten* [enchanted, fallen in love] by her when he saw her.

They came and saw where he *abode* ["lived", uncommon in modern English]. He *abode* the result of a political storm ["endured", also uncommon]. She *abided by* [accepted] the decision of the jury. They have always *abided by* the law [behaved in accordance with the law].

Long ago he *rode* away. I have never *ridden* a horse. He *strode* [paced] quickly out of the room. I've *stridden* (or *strode*) through the whole house. [However, note that the past participle of "stride" is rarely used in contemporary English.]

VERBS WITH -OVE
IN THE PAST TENSE

Several verbs change from -ive or -eave to -ove in the past tense:

> **drive** – **drove** – **driven**
> **strive** – **strove** (or *strived*) – **striven** (or *strived*)
> **weave** (cloth, threads, etc.) – **wove** – **woven**

The verb "weave" has another possible meaning: "to move quickly and change direction often to avoid hitting things that are in the way". In this sense it is usually used as a regular verb (with past tense and past participle "weaved").

There is a tendency for the verb "strive" to become regularized in modern English, but this may be marked as an error by some English teachers, and the traditional form ("strove", "striven") is still more common in writing, so I recommend sticking to it.

There are two more verbs that have a similar irregular form, but the regular form is much more common and, therefore, preferable: "heave" (meaning "lift" or "rise") and "thrive". They can follow the patterns "heave – hove – hove" and "thrive – throve – thriven", respectively, but I recommend using the regular forms "heaved" and "thrived".

There are two rather archaic verbs that follow the same pattern. I mention them for the sake of completeness, but it is not necessary to memorize them:

> **shrive** [receive or give confession]
> – **shrove** or **shrived** – **shriven** or **shrived**
> **rive** [break apart, cleave] – **rove** – **riven**

Finally, the past tense of "dive" is commonly "dove" in American English, but it may be considered an Americanism in the UK:

> **dive** – **dove** (AmE) or **dived** – **dived**

The form "dived" is perfectly acceptable in American English as well, and as such it is usually preferable.

PATTERNS -EED -ED -ED
AND RELATED

A common pattern among irregular English verbs is characterized by the change /iːd/ → /ɛd/ in pronunciation in the past tense and past participle. There are two types of such verbs. Those ending with -eed are as follows:

> **bleed – bled – bled**
> **breed – bred – bred**
> **feed – fed – fed**
> **speed – sped** *or* **speeded – sped** *or* **speeded**

Both "speeded" and "sped" can be used as the past tense and past participle of "speed", but "sped" is somewhat more common.

There are two verbs ending with -ead that follow the same pattern:

> **lead – led – led**
> **read – read** /rɛd/ **– read** /rɛd/

These verbs are a common source of spelling mistakes. Many native speakers incorrectly spell the past tense of "lead" as "lead", probably because the name of the chemical element "lead" (Pb) is pronounced /lɛd/, but the only correct spelling of the past tense of "lead" is "led". On the other hand, the past tense of "read" is never spelled "red"; you must recognize the correct pronunciation from the context.

Finally, "flee" follows a similar pattern:

> **flee – fled – fled**

There is one additional verb we should discuss here. The verb "plead" (meaning "to beg" or "to state something in court") has traditionally been regular, but there has been a tendency in American English to use it irregularly (as the form given in parentheses):

> **plead** – **pleaded** (or "pled") – **pleaded** (or "pled")

Nevertheless, many speakers still consider "pled" to be wrong, so it is advisable for a non-native speaker to avoid it and use "pleaded" instead.

EXAMPLES

His hand *bled* because he cut himself. Many animals are *bred* for their meat. I *fed* my cat. The suspect *sped* away from the crime scene.

Hannibal *led* his army through the Alps. She *read* /rɛd/ a book about it yesterday.

Roman legionaries *fled* into the woods.

The burglar *pleaded* guilty.

Pattern -EAVE -EFT -EFT

There is only one common English verb that follows the pattern -eave /iːv/ → -eft /ɛft/, namely:

leave – **left** – **left**

Another, much less common verb that follows the same pattern is:

bereave [to deprive of] – **bereft** – **bereft**

For example:

He lost all his money and was bereft of hope.

However, "bereave" has also another, more common meaning, which is "take away by death". Its regular past participle ("bereaved") is normally only used as a noun in this sense, referring to those who have lost a beloved person:

I expressed my condolences to the bereaved.

Finally, the verb "cleave", meaning "to split something in two using a sharp tool or weapon" may or may not follow the same pattern:

cleave – **cleft**, **cleaved**, **clove**, or **clave** – **cleft**, **cleaved**, or **cloven** (see below!)

Considering the number of possible forms, this verb is probably the record holder in English. The past tense form "clave" /kleɪv/ is now considered obsolete, although we can still find it in biblical references. Also note that "clove(n)" is pronounced /ˈkləʊv(n)/ in the UK and /ˈkloʊv(n)/ in the US.

One relatively common expression with "cleave" used in historical contexts is "cleft in twain" ("twain" being an archaic form of "two"), e.g.

O Hamlet, thou hast cleft my heart in twain!
(from Shakespeare's Hamlet)

PATTERN -OKE -OKEN

There are only three verbs with -oke in the past tense and -oken in the past participle:

> **break – broke – broken**
> **speak – spoke – spoken**
> **wake – woke – woken**

The verb "awake" follows the same pattern as "wake", but the situation is further complicated by the existence of the regular verb "awaken" (which means the same). Compare:

awake – awoke – awoken
awaken – awakened – awakened

EXAMPLES

I *broke* my leg. They have *broken* the record. We *spoke* about it earlier. You have never *spoken* about it. I *woke* early this morning. Have you already *woken* up?

I *awoke* in the middle of the night. I was *awoken* by something. That means I was *awakened* by it.

VERBS WITH -UCK

There two verbs with -uck in the past simple and past participle:

> **stick – stuck – stuck**
> **strike – struck – struck**

The verb "sneak" is traditionally regular, but an irregular form is becoming increasingly more common:

> **sneak – sneaked** (or *snuck*) **– sneaked** (or *snuck*)

While the form "snuck" is so widespread that it should not be considered an error, the form "sneaked" is still a safer option, especially in a formal environment.

EXAMPLES

The glue *stuck* to my finger. We've been *stuck* here for hours. Her idea *struck* me as odd. Their house has been *struck* by a lightning several times. The child *sneaked* out of the class. It has *sneaked* out. (*or, informally, "snuck"*)

Pattern -ow -ew -own

There are four verbs following the pattern -ow -ew -own:

    blow – blew – blown
    grow – grew – grown
    know – knew – known
    throw – threw – thrown

The verb "draw" follows a similar pattern:

    draw – drew – drawn

The verb "withdraw" follows the same pattern (withdraw – withdrew – withdrawn) because "with-" is a prefix meaning "against" or "away", as in "withstand" or "withhold".

Finally, the verb "fly" follows a similar pattern, even though its present tense does not end with -ow:

    fly – flew – flown

These forms should not be confused with the verb "flow", which is regular: flow – flowed – flowed.

It *blew* my mind. A political row /raʊ/ has *blown* up in the parliament. Scientists *grew* vegetables in Martian soil. My son has *grown* up. She *knew* all the answers. The results are not *known*. He *threw* a stone. The message has *thrown* me off.

The girl *drew* a house. The house was *hand-drawn*.

I flew to Madrid last night, but I have never *flown* with that company before.

PATTERNS -OW -OWED -OWN AND -EW -EWED -EWN

There is one verb with the past participle always formed by adding -n instead of -ed:

show – showed – shown

In the following cases, the regular "-ed" form of the past participle is acceptable, but the irregular form is more common (and therefore preferable):

> **sow** [spread seeds] – **sowed** – **sown**
> **hew** [cut] – **hewed** – **hewn**
> **sew** [use a needle] – **sewed** – **sewn**
> **strew** [scatter] – **strewed** – **strewn**

Note that "sew" (unlike "hew" /hjuː/ and "strew" /struː/) is pronounced exactly the same as "sow", namely /soʊ/ in American English and /səʊ/ in British English.

Finally, there is one verb for which both forms are common, but the regular one is more common:

> **mow** [cut grass] – **mowed** – **mowed** or **mown**

EXAMPLES

The children have *shown* great interest in science. We reap what we have *sown*. They have *hewn* (or *hewed*) a wooden frame. I have *sewn*

(or *sewed*) up the trouser leg. It was autumn, and the ground was *strewn* (or *strewed*) with leaves.

I have *mowed* (or *mown*) the front lawn.

PATTERN -EAR -ORE -ORN

A small class of verbs is characterized by the pattern -ear -ore -orn (-ear pronounced as /ɛr/ in AmE and /ɛə/ in BrE):

> **bear – bore – borne** or **born** (*see below*)
> **swear – swore – sworn**
> **tear – tore – torn**
> **wear – wore – worn**

The past participle of "bear" is "borne" in all senses unrelated to giving birth, in which case it is "born" (see the example sentences at the end of this section).

The verb shear (pronounced as /ʃɪr/ in AmE and /ʃɪə/ in BrE) follows a somewhat similar pattern:

shear – **sheared** (or *shore*) – **shorn**

The past participle "shore" is rare and should be avoided by non-native speakers.

EXAMPLES

The whole country *bore* the consequences of the politician's decision. They have *borne* it with patience. Flu is an *airborne* disease. She was *born* in 1996.

The knight *swore* loyalty to the king. I could have *sworn* I had already seen him somewhere.

She *tore* my letter apart. I am *torn* between these two options. He *wore* a formal suit. The button has been *worn* out by constant use.

The shepherd *sheared* his sheep. Now they are all *shorn*.

ADJECTIVES WITH -EN

The following adjectives look deceptively like past participles of the type mentioned in the previous sections, but they should never be used as verbs:

> **drunken**, **molten**, **proven**, **shaven**,
> **shrunken**, **sunken**

Here are a few examples of correct usage:

> a *drunken* driver
> *molten* metal
> a *proven* fact
> a *shaven* head
> a *shrunken* T-shirt
> a *sunken* boat

With the exception of "proven", none of the adjectives above should be used to form the past perfect of the corresponding verbs. Sentences like "I have drunken all the wine" or "the boat has sunken" are incorrect; the correct form is "I have drunk all the wine" and "the boat has sunk", respectively.

There is a controversy surrounding "proven", which is becoming increasingly used as the past participle of "prove". Such usage is often frowned upon by traditional grammarians, especially in British English. Using the form "have proved" is a safer option.

MODAL VERBS

To conclude this book, we will take a quick look at modal verbs in the past tense. There are four modal verbs that have, at least formally, a simple past form (which is also used separately as another modal verb):

> **can – could**
> **may – might**
> **shall – should**
> **will – would**

Of these, only "could" is still used as the past tense of "can", as in

> He could not arrive on time yesterday.

This leads to possible ambiguities. In a sentence such as

> I could eat a horse.

it is not clear whether the intended meaning is "I would be able to eat a horse" or "I was able to eat a horse". Nonetheless, if there is no indication that the action took place in the past, the intended meaning is usually "would be able to", as in the idiom above, which means "I am very hungry".

The other three past simple forms ("might", "should", "would") are not used to express the past tense in modern English; they are used as modal verbs in their own right.

To express the idea of a past action of a modal verb other than "can", use the following construction instead:

modal verb + have + past participle

Here are a few examples:

> He could have done better than he did.
> She may have been there yesterday.
> They might have found out.
> We should have anticipated this.
> You would have thought that he'd be there.

Because "shall" and "will" are used to express the future tense, it would not make sense for "shall have" and "will have" to refer to an action that has already happened. Instead, they refer to *finished* actions in the future (the so called *future perfect* tense):

> They will have done it by tomorrow.
> I shall have written the report before noon.

The verbs "must", "ought to", "had better", and "need" can also be combined with "have" to refer to the past:

> He must have earned a lot of money.
> It ought to have been done.
> You'd better have done your homework!
> She needn't have done that.

(but "did not need to do" is more common in contemporary English; remember that "need" can be used as an ordinary verb).

Finally, "dare" and "used to" are never combined with "have" ("dare have done" and "used to have done" are not idiomatic). The past tense of "dare" is "dared", which can be used as a modal verb in negative sentences, e.g.

> I dared not enter the room.
> (= *I didn't dare to enter the room.*)

Historically, the past tense of "dare" was "durst" (so the sentence above would read "I durst not enter the room"), but this form is rarely used in modern English.

Final remarks

Thank you for your interest in this book. I hope you have enjoyed the process of learning about irregular English verbs. If you liked the book, you might also be interested in my book entitled *Most Common Mistakes in English: An English Learner's Guide*:

jakubmarian.com/english-mistakes/

Several other books on issues English learners must face are currently being prepared, and a lot of freely available information can be found at:

jakubmarian.com

You can also follow me on:

Facebook: facebook.com/JakubMarian

Google+:   google.com/+JakubMarian

Twitter: twitter.com/JakubMarian

Mailing list: jakubmarian.com/mailing-list/

Should you find any mistake in the book, please, send me an email to

jakub.marian@jakubmarian.com

Alphabetical Index

Made in United States
North Haven, CT
15 May 2022

19187445R00059